THIS JOURNAL BELONGS TO:

ABRAMS NOTERIE, NEW YORK

NEW DAY

New year, new you, new…day! Instead of wasting time with resolutions today (those are *so* last year), let's talk about all the fun new stuff you're going to do *this* year.

What do you hope to have accomplished one year from now?

_____

_____

_____

_____

_____

_____

_____

_____

JANUARY 2ND

SCIENCE FICTION DAY

To celebrate today, write about a science fiction phenomenon that you'd like to experience in real life (Time travel? Meeting an alien?).

BARE YOUR SOUL DAY

Only three days into the year and the time has come to fully put your trust in this journal. Reveal your innermost feelings about, well, anything. You might just feel lighter afterwards—and hey, journals can't spill secrets.

TRIVIA DAY

Get excited, info-lovers!

Make it your business to learn some fun facts today.
Or even just one fun fact! Then write 'em down.

_____

_____

_____

_____

_____

_____

_____

_____

_____

_____

_____

BiRD DAY

Grab your binoculars! And if you don't have time to birdwatch today—that's okay!

Just draw the most colorful bird you can imagine here.

CUDDLE UP DAY

Who or what should you cuddle up with? Well, that's up to you. Try and get in a good #cuddlesesh or two today.

How does cuddling make you feel? Claustrophobic? Happy? Nostalgic? Warm? #allthefeels

_____

_____

_____

_____

_____

BOBBLEHEAD DAY

No, you're not absentmindedly shaking your head back and forth—deep down you must know it's Bobblehead Day.

If you were to start a bobblehead collection, who would the first bobblehead be? The second? The third?

_____

_____

_____

_____

_____

_____

_____

_____

BUBBLE BATH DAY

One week into the new year? That's the perfect time to treat yourself to a soak!

Brainstorm some ways you can bring that bubble bath relaxation feeling into your everyday life for the rest of the year.

_____

_____

_____

_____

_____

_____

_____

_____

PLAY GOD DAY

Okay, let's not go overboard. Think small-scale:

What would you change in your life if you had total control for one day?

_____

_____

_____

_____

_____

_____

_____

_____

PECULIAR PEOPLE DAY

Take this opportunity to celebrate the peculiar people in your life (probably everyone you know has at least *some* weird in them).

Who's the most peculiar person you know, and why? And what's the most peculiar thing about YOU?

_____

_____

_____

_____

_____

FREAK
FLAG

_____

_____

_____

_____

_____

_____

STEP IN A PUDDLE DAY

It's pretty obvious what you have to do to celebrate:
Step 1: Find a puddle. Step 2: Step in said puddle
and splash around.

You could celebrate that way, or list your favorite
rainy-day activities below.

_____

_____

_____

_____

_____

_____

_____

_____

AMATEUR DETECTIVE DAY

Can you use your sleuthing skills to figure out what day today is?

Clue #1: It's an easy case to crack.

Clue #2: You hardly need to be a professional.

Clue #3: The answer is literally at the top of the page.

Elementary, my dear Watson! It's _____ Day.

What's the mystery you're most fascinated by in life?

_____

_____

_____

_____

_____

_____

_____

_____

_____

SKEPTICS DAY

Hmm, not so sure about today? You've come to the right place. You don't have to believe everything you're told, and a healthy dose of skepticism should be encouraged—especially today.

What are some things you're naturally skeptical about?

_____

_____

_____

_____

_____

DRESS UP YOUR PET DAY

Let's make this as painless as possible for our animal friends—instead of actually forcing your dog into a raincoat or your lizard into a chef's hat, draw a picture of your pet—or any animal in your life—dressed up.

WIKIPEDIA DAY

Wikipedia! The place where many of us get *a lot* of our info in the modern age. We all should probably check out some other sources sometime…but not today.

Spend some time today doing what you probably do on so many other days: Get lost in a Wikipedia hole. Chart your progress jumping from article to article here, and then review the chain. Look how much you've learned!

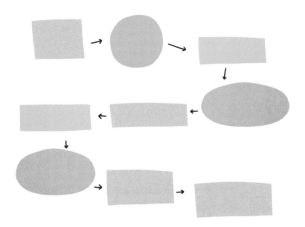

NOTHING DAY

Your mission, should you choose to accept it:
Do nothing today (except like, breathe, eat, drink
water, etc.). Don't even write or draw anything
here, because, hey, nothing means nothing.
See you tomorrow.

KID INVENTORS DAY

You probably had an idea for a super cool invention when you were a kid. What was it? What did it look like?

Do you still wish your invention could come to life?

_____

_____

_____

_____

_____

_____

THESAURUS DAY

What a great, awesome, fantastic, marvelous, terrific, wonderful day!

Pick your favorite word and look up all its synonyms and antonyms. List your favorite three new words below and add them to your vocabulary.

_____

_____

_____

_____

_____

_____

_____

_____

POPCORN DAY

For the love of all that's buttery and salty! You're more than welcome to make and eat some delicious popcorn whenever you want today. *Yum.*

What's your favorite popcorn seasoning or mix-in combo? Caramel? Hot sauce? Garlic powder? M&Ms?

_____

_____

_____

_____

_____

_____

_____

CHALLENGE AUTHORITY DAY

Go to a local protest for something you believe in or politely tell your boss to get their own double espresso today!

What's one way you challenge authority, big or small scale, every day?

_____

_____

_____

_____

_____

_____

_____

_____

_____

_____

HUGGING DAY

Hope you've been stretching those arms! You don't have to go around hugging everyone you see, but definitely give some hugs to your loved ones and maybe a tree, if you're into the environment.

Who did you hug today, and why?

ANSWER YOUR CAT'S QUESTIONS DAY

Today's is your cat's lucky day. If your cat could talk, what questions would they ask?

If you're catless, feel free to skip today, or ask and answer a few imaginary questions from ANY cat, ever. Ready, set, meow!

HANDWRITING DAY

Ol' John Hancock is rolling in his grave (in a good way) today. Practice your penmanship below. Try changing it up, too!

COMPLIMENT DAY

Get your flattery skills in order. Compliment as much as you can today (but only if you mean it) and accept all compliments with a smile.

What is the best compliment you've ever received?

_____

_____

_____

_____

_____

_____

_____

OPPOSITE DAY

Fourth Grade You is probably squealing in excitement, because the holiday you used to toss around the lunch table is finally REAL (well, in this journal, at least).

What are some viewpoints that are in direct opposition to some of yours? Do you think there could be any opportunities to find some common ground?

_____

_____

_____

_____

_____

_____

_____

_____

NO DAY

NUH UH NAH NO HOW ABOUT NO NOPE

Think about all the times you've said "yes" to a favor or an event without really thinking it through, or because you felt obligated, and later wished you'd just said "no." Describe some of those instances (and remember that feeling for the future).

_____

_____

_____

_____

_____

_____

_____

_____

_____

CHOCOLATE CAKE DAY

If you lo-o-ove chocolate cake, it's time to grab a fork. Definitely eat a slice today, or record your favorite recipe, or describe your favorite decadent dessert below.

KAZOO DAY

You could spend the day playing the kazoo, naturally. But if playing the kazoo all day just isn't feasible, at least take a few minutes to describe your favorite musical relic from childhood.

_____

_____

_____

_____

_____

_____

_____

_____

_____

PUZZLE DAY

There are all kinds of puzzles out there: Jigsaw, crossword, Sudoku—just to name a few. Indulge in some puzzle play today; it's good for the brain.

For an extra brain boost, craft a few anagram puzzles below. The harder, the better!

_____

_____

_____

_____

_____

_____

_____

_____

RÉSUMÉ DAY

Use today to polish up your résumé. It might not be very fun, but it *is* pretty necessary. You'll thank January 30th the next time you apply for a job.

Now take a few minutes to record your current position and your dream job below.

YAD SDRAWKCAB

You guessed it, it's Backwards Day! You could celebrate by writing or saying everything backwards, or you could take some time to look back over the past month.

What would you re-do this January if you could?

_____

_____

_____

_____

_____

_____

_____

_____

_____

_____

WORK NAKED DAY

Put all of your opinions and ideas out there—no qualms, let it all out.

What was the best thing about metaphorically working naked? And the worst?

Would you ever really want to go to work in your birthday suit?

_____

_____

_____

_____

_____

_____

_____

_____

_____

NO COFFEE DAY

You can do it. No coffee today! It won't kill you, though it may feel like it will. If you're feeling really bold, make a resolution to go without coffee one day a week from now on!

How'd it go? Were you crankier than usual?

_____

_____

_____

_____

_____

_____

WISH UPON A STAR DAY

You've got some wishing to do! You'll have to wait until nighttime to really celebrate, but to prepare, brainstorm some of your wishes here.

Remember, you can only pick one when the time comes.

_____

_____

_____

_____

_____

_____

_____

_____

_____

THANK A MAIL CARRIER DAY

Snow, rain, heat, gloom of night…nothing stops those dedicated mail carriers from bringing you bills, takeout menus, and wedding invitations. Don't they deserve a wholehearted thank you?

What's the best piece of mail you've ever received?

_____

_____

_____

_____

_____

_____

_____

_____

SUDS DAY

Nothing is better than letting things soak—whether it's you or a pile of dirty dishes.

Today is the day for taking your time, letting things soak in. What do you notice more when you slow down?

_____

_____

_____

_____

_____

_____

_____

SHOWER REFLECTION DAY

Enjoy the peace and quiet during today's shower. The shower is a great place to think, so where are all of the places your mind wanders to during your shower?

_____

_____

_____

_____

_____

_____

_____

_____

_____

SEND A CARD TO A FRIEND DAY

Sending mail is just as fun as getting it. This one is easy to celebrate: Get a card, write a note in it, affix a stamp on the envelope, and mail it!

Who did you write to and why?

_____

_____

_____

_____

_____

_____

_____

_____

_____

_____

FLY A KITE DAY

Depending on where you live, it might be a little cold for this activity—but that's okay, you can cheat.

To celebrate, design your dream kite here. And fantasize about it until spring.

BAGEL DAY

Your mission, should you choose to accept it (and you really should, unless you have a gluten allergy): Eat a bagel. A delicious, doughy bagel, with whatever you want on top.

Before you dig in, take a minute to draw a detailed diagram, with all toppings, spreads, etc., labeled here. You'll want to remember this bagel.

UMBRELLA DAY

Do you have a favorite umbrella? Today's the day to break it out (but not inside—that's bad luck).

When was the last time you were caught in the rain *without* your trusty umbrella? Recount every soggy detail below!

_____

_____

_____

_____

_____

_____

_____

_____

_____

_____

DON'T CRY OVER SPILLED MILK DAY

What are some things you let go today because they were ultimately out of your control?

_____

_____

_____

_____

_____

_____

_____

_____

REMINISCING DAY

Take a few moments today to look back on some of your happiest memories. Reminisce alone, with friends, with family...however you want.

What is your first memory? Details, please.

_____

_____

_____

_____

_____

_____

_____

GET A DIFFERENT NAME DAY

As Shakespeare once asked, what's in a name? Would you still be you if you were called something else?

Brainstorm a list of possible new names here, then narrow it down to one. If you had gone by this other name, how might your life be different?

ORGAN DONOR DAY

Happy Val—oh, wait, no, that's not what we're celebrating today. What are your thoughts and feelings about organ donation?

CAViTY DAY

Okay, this isn't exactly a fun one, but it IS necessary. You know what you have to do: Make some cavity-avoiding resolutions here for the rest of the year.

_____

_____

_____

_____

_____

_____

_____

_____

_____

DO A GROUCH A FAVOR DAY

You can probably find a grouch or two in your everyday life—and not just on Sesame Street. Hard as it may be (grouches are grouchy, after all), do that person a favor today.

Who is the biggest grouch in your life?

_____

_____

_____

_____

_____

_____

_____

_____

_____

RANDOM ACTS OF KINDNESS DAY

What are some of the random acts of kindness you did today or could do in the future?

_____

_____

_____

_____

_____

_____

_____

_____

DRINK WINE DAY

You probably shouldn't spend *all* day drinking wine, but definitely partake in sipping a little Adult Grape Juice if you can (or real grape juice, if you're not of age).

Test out some new wines (or juices!), and describe them here.

_____

_____

_____

_____

_____

_____

_____

SLEEP LATE DAY

It's the best day of the year. Your one mission today is to sleep in!

What are the pros and cons of sleeping in? Are you an early bird or someone who always hits snooze?

_____

_____

_____

_____

_____

_____

zzzz

_____

WRITE IN PENCIL DAY

Hope your pencils are sharpened!

Use the space below to write a "dear diary" entry about your day. In pencil. Obviously.

QUESTION EVERYTHING DAY

Who? What? Where? Why? When?

...and how?

A little curiosity never hurt anyone (except that one cat).

What are some questions you've ALWAYS wanted the answers to?

_____

_____

_____

_____

_____

_____

_____

_____

_____

_____

_____

BE HUMBLE DAY

Now, don't totally deny your awesomeness or anything, but just remember to be a little modest as you go about your day today.

What are the pros and cons of being modest, in your humble (wink, wink) opinion?

TOAST DAY

Use today to prepare (or give) a toast to/about one of your friends.

Use the space below to draft your future toast. And don't worry if you have stage fright—you'll crush it.

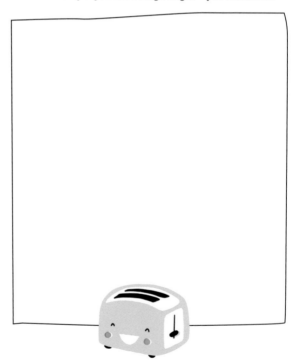

TiP DAY

Here's a tip: no man is an island, and everyone needs a little helping hand once in a while.

What's a great life tip you've received recently? And what's one you've given? Money counts!

_____

_____

_____

_____

_____

_____

AFRAID OF CHANGE?
leave it here!

BUNDLE UP DAY

Brr, this holiday is here just in time.

What are some things that make you warm inside or out?

_____

_____

_____

_____

_____

_____

_____

_____

FAIRY TALE DAY

Once upon a time, it was February 26th.

To celebrate, start your own fairy tale here
or make a list of your favorite fairy tales.

_____

_____

_____

_____

_____

_____

_____

POLAR BEAR DAY

Polar bears are so cool—literally.

What is the coldest place you've ever traveled to?
Would you want to live in the Arctic with the polar
bears if you could?

_____

_____

_____

_____

_____

_____

_____

ZONE OUT DAY

...

...

...Oops! Just getting a head start on zoning out...

Take some time today to let your mind wander and see where it takes you.

What did you think about?

_____

_____

_____

_____

_____

LEAP DAY

Most years, this day doesn't even exist—so make the most of it while its here. Do things you've always wanted to do but haven't gotten around to, because today you've been given the gift of time!

How did you spend your Leap Day?

_____

_____

_____

_____

_____

_____

_____

PLAN A SOLO VACATION DAY

Two months into the year—it's time to plan a vacation to get away from it all. What are you waiting for? Get planning!

Use this space to keep track of your trip research or to create your dream itinerary.

_____

_____

_____

_____

_____

_____

OLD STUFF DAY

Celebrate all the old stuff cluttering up your life today.

What are some things you could stand to clean out of your home or work space? What's holding you back?

_____

_____

_____

_____

_____

_____

_____

WORLD WILDLIFE DAY

To celebrate, learn something about wildlife today! Watch *Planet Earth*, read *Nat Geo*, or just do a little Googling.

What did you learn? And how can you help wildlife conservation efforts worldwide?

_____

_____

_____

_____

_____

_____

_____

_____

DAY OF UNPLUGGING

Unplug today as much as you can. No phones. No computers. No TV. The list goes on…and on…and on…

How did being unplugged make you feel?

_____

_____

_____

_____

_____

_____

_____

_____

_____

LEARN WHAT YOUR NAME MEANS DAY

Plug back in and spend some time Googling today.

So...what does your name mean?

Write an acrostic poem with your name here.

_____

_____

_____

_____

_____

_____

_____

_____

FROZEN FOOD DAY

Frozen food might not always be good for you, but it can be really tasty and convenient.

What are your top five favorite items from the frozen food aisle?

_____

_____

_____

_____

_____

_____

_____

_____

CEREAL DAY

Spoons ready! There are tons of cereals out there just waiting for you to taste them. To celebrate, eat cereal for *at least* one meal.

What's your favorite cereal? Least favorite?

_____

_____

_____

_____

_____

_____

_____

WOMEN'S DAY

Today is the day to celebrate all the women in your life. Who are some of your favorite women, and how do they inspire you or otherwise touch your life?

_____

_____

_____

_____

_____

_____

_____

_____

_____

PANIC DAY

Let's *not* celebrate by, well, panicking! Instead, let's indulge in some self-examination. What makes you panic? What does it feel like when you panic about something, and how do you eventually calm down?

_____

_____

_____

_____

_____

_____

_____

_____

_____

_____

COOL AS
A CUCUMBER

AWESOMENESS DAY

It's pretty simple: Today is the day to really revel in awesomeness.

What was the most AWESOME thing you witnessed today? And what is the most AWESOME thing about you?

CRAFTING DAY

Get the glue and pom-poms ready! Even if you don't think you're creative or artsy, try to indulge in some craft time today. It's good for the soul.

What is your favorite crafting activity from childhood?

_____

_____

_____

_____

_____

PLANT A SEED DAY!

Spring is almost here! Green thumb or not, do your part by planting a seed today—or at least buy a flower that you can re-pot later. You can do it!

What did you plant? And where did you plant it?

_____

_____

_____

_____

_____

_____

_____

JEWEL DAY

Emeralds and sapphires and rubies, oh my!
Celebrate today by looking up the backstory of
your birthstone.

What is it and does it fit your personality?

_____

_____

_____

_____

_____

_____

_____

_____

_____

_____

_____

_____

_____

PI DAY

You know what that means: It's math time. Or, you could interpret today phonetically, and celebrate pie instead of pi. It's really up to you.

To celebrate both, make up a recipe for Pi Pie, and record it here for posterity.

π!

EVERYTHING YOU THINK IS WRONG DAY

Womp, womp. Do you ever stop to look at an argument from the other side? Today is the perfect day to question yourself.

What is something you once turned out to be wrong about?

_____

_____

_____

_____

_____

_____

_____

_____

EVERYTHING YOU DO IS RIGHT DAY

Today, take a little time to inflate your ego. Feel confident about doing your thing today; don't second-guess things—just trust that you're right.

What makes you feel most confident about yourself?

_____

_____

_____

_____

_____

_____

_____

SUBMARINE DAY

Power up Google and learn fun facts about submarines! Eat a submarine (the sandwich, that is), or visit a submarine museum today!

What would be the best and worst things about living under water in a submarine?

_____

_____

_____

_____

_____

_____

_____

AWKWARD MOMENTS DAY

Yikes. This is...awkward. Because awkwardness is what today's all about.

Describe your most cringe-worthy moment ever.

_____

_____

_____

_____

_____

_____

_____

_____

_____

_____

_____

_____

_____

_____

LET'S LAUGH DAY

Ha! Teehee! Ahaha! Hehe! Seek out humor today and jot down some things that have made you laugh recently.

How would you describe your laugh?

_____

_____

_____

_____

_____

_____

_____

_____

_____

HA!

STORYTELLING DAY

Get your imagination ready and dedicate today to storytelling.

What is your all-time favorite story to tell? To read?

_____

_____

_____

_____

_____

_____

_____

_____

_____

COMMON COURTESY DAY

Celebrate the little things today; the common courtesies we probably take for granted most of the time.

What are the common courtesies you engage in every day? And which ones would you like to make more of an effort to participate in?

_____

_____

_____

_____

_____

_____

GOOF OFF DAY

I hope the authority figure in your life has a sense of humor today!

Goof off whenever and wherever you can today (within reason)! Have you ever gotten in trouble for goofing off? What happened?

_____

_____

_____

_____

_____

_____

_____

_____

PUPPY DAY

PUPPIES! What could be cuter? Not a whole lot.

Volunteer at a shelter. Pet some puppies walking down the street. Look at pictures of puppies online. Watch *101 Dalmatians*.

Write about your favorite dog here, real or fictional (Lassie counts!).

GET A PUPPY DAY

After celebrating puppies yesterday, you're probably feeling pretty drunk on puppies today. You might even be thinking that it's about time you get a puppy of your own.

What pet are you pining after? Make a pet ownership pros/cons list here to help you decide.

EXPLETIVE DAY

#$@*&%!

Oh #$@&%*! Curse your heart out today, then take some time to think about your favorite expletive and figure out what can you sub it with when you're in a situation where you can't curse.

What is it? What are its best substitutes?

_____

_____

_____

_____

_____

_____

_____

_____

_____

MAKE UP YOUR OWN HOLIDAY DAY

How meta.

What's your made-up holiday? How do you suggest we celebrate?

Let's do it!

_____

_____

_____

_____

_____

_____

YES DAY

YAS!

MAIS OUI!

YES

UH-HUH

HECK YEAH!

Take a cue from Shonda Rhimes and Jim Carrey (who knew those two had anything in common?) and say "yes" today. You never know where it might lead you.

Do you want to say "yes" to more stuff?

_____

_____

_____

_____

_____

_____

_____

SOMETHING ON A STICK DAY

Some classic something-on-a-stick foods: Shish kebabs, ice pops, lollipops…

What's your favorite food on a stick? What memory does it remind you of?

_____

_____

_____

_____

_____

_____

_____

_____

_____

_____

_____

SMOKE AND MIRRORS DAY

The phrase typically refers to a magician's ability to deceive an audience using smoke and mirrors, but how do you encounter smoke and mirrors in your everyday life?

TAKE A WALK IN THE PARK DAY

This is an easy one: Take a walk in a park today.

What's your favorite way to commune with nature?

CRAYON DAY

Time to throw it back to childhood.

What's your favorite crayon color? Come up with a creative alternative name for it here (write it in crayon if you can!).

ONE-CENT DAY

What would you buy if you saved up every spare penny that crossed your path for a year? And what do you think should only cost one cent?

_____

_____

_____

_____

_____

_____

_____

_____

_____

_____

_____

PEANUT BUTTER AND JELLY DAY

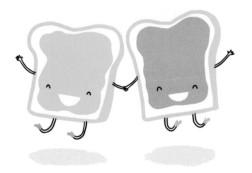

Obviously, you should celebrate by eating a PB&J sandwich! If you're allergic to PB or don't care for J, jot down some other food or condiment combos that are a match made in heaven.

FIND A RAINBOW DAY

Leprechauns of the world—and everyone else, too—rejoice! And look hard for a rainbow today.

Bask in the awe of the rainbow(s) and any other natural phenomena you see today. Which natural wonder do you love the most?

_____

_____

_____

_____

_____

_____

_____

_____

_____

_____

TELL A LIE DAY

Today you'll find out if everyone else has their B.S. meters turned on. Don't trust anyone.

What did you lie about today? What's the biggest lie you've ever told?

_____

_____

_____

_____

_____

NO BULL!

READ A ROAD MAP DAY

How retro.

To celebrate, make a list all of the cities, states, or countries you've been to. What route could you use to get to all of those spots in one trip?

_____

_____

_____

_____

_____

_____

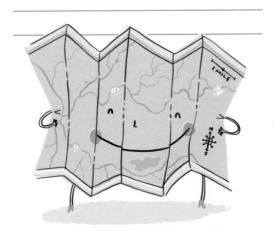

PLAN YOUR EPITAPH DAY

Sure, this day is kind of dark, but maybe it's good to confront our mortality once in a while. So what will your legacy be?

Draft your epitaph here.

_____

_____

_____

_____

_____

_____

_____

_____

NO HOUSEWORK DAY

Let those dishes and dust bunnies pile up.

Does it feel good, or are you just itching to clean up? What is your absolute least favorite chore? Are there any that you find kind of relaxing?

_____

_____

_____

_____

_____

_____

_____

_____

_____

BURN IT ALL DOWN DAY

Do you ever feel so frustrated (with work, your significant other, the world, etc.) that you just want to burn it all down? Theoretically, that is. Not literally.

Instead of burning anything, how about you just vent here?

_____

_____

_____

_____

_____

_____

CHERISH AN ANTIQUE DAY

Antiques have long pre-dated you, which is pretty cool when you think about it.

What's your most cherished antique? What are the memories you associate with it?

_____

_____

_____

_____

_____

_____

_____

_____

_____

_____

SiBLiNGS DAY

What's your favorite sibling story? If you don't have
a sibling, who is someone that you consider to be
like a brother or sister to you?

Also, don't forget to call your sibling today!

_____

_____

_____

_____

_____

_____

_____

_____

_____

_____

_____

_____

_____

_____

PET DAY

And now to celebrate a different kind of family: The animal kind!

Write about your first pet here.

_____

_____

_____

_____

_____

_____

_____

GRiLLED CHEESE DAY

Yummmmmmm...

Go ahead and feast if you're a gooey, melty cheese fan. Since grilled cheese is a classic kids' menu dish, think back to a time when that selection was your go-to. What's your favorite "kid" food?

CHEESE!

SCRABBLE DAY

Open up the board game closet! Try playing Scrabble with some different rules in place—like playing with only the letters of your name. What words (aside from your name) can you make out of these letters?

A.

L.

B.

R.

H A. M.

A.

C. I. N. N. O.

L. O.

REACH AS HIGH AS YOU CAN DAY

Aside from reaching for something on a high shelf today, to celebrate, write about your loftiest dream or goal. How will you achieve it?

_____

_____

_____

_____

_____

_____

THAT SUCKS DAY

Sometimes, things just…suck. And today is about embracing the suckage.

What sucked about today?

_____

_____

_____

_____

_____

_____

_____

_____

_____

_____

WEAR PAJAMAS TO WORK DAY

Time to get comfy! Your instructions are clear. Wear your PJs to work or school today. And if you can't, slip into them the second you get home.

Draw a quick sketch of your ultimate sleep gear here.

HAIKU POETRY DAY

All you need to know for today is: 5, 7, 5.

To celebrate, educate yourself about the art of haiku. And then write your own haiku poem—about anything you want.

DREAM DAY

Dreams can be wacky, scary, thrilling...and sometimes they can be so fun we don't want to wake up.

What's the weirdest dream you've ever had? Scariest? Happiest?

_____

_____

_____

_____

_____

_____

_____

_____

_____

_____

GARLIC DAY

Vampires, beware! To celebrate this stinky holiday, brainstorm all the possible uses for garlic—in food or elsewhere—below.

_____

_____

_____

_____

_____

_____

_____

_____

_____

_____

_____

DO I OFFEND?

LOOK-ALIKE DAY

To celebrate, seek out your celebrity doppelganger IRL or by scouring pics online.

What would you do if you met your look-alike, face-to-face?

_____

_____

_____

_____

_____

_____

_____

_____

KINDERGARTEN DAY

Reach back in your memory and think about little you at the tender age of 5 (or 4, or 6, or whenever you started kindergarten).

What was your first day of kindergarten like?

_____

_____

_____

_____

_____

_____

JELLY BEAN DAY

Be glad we don't live in the wizarding world of Harry Potter, because no one wants to eat an earwax-flavored jelly bean.

Don't *just* gorge yourself on the candy today—instead, brainstorm some really *out there* jelly bean flavors.

PICNIC DAY

You may not have time for a picnic today, so let's just plan for the future.

What would go in your ideal picnic basket? What would you use as a picnic blanket? And most importantly…where will your next picnic be?

_____

_____

_____

_____

_____

_____

_____

POEM IN YOUR POCKET DAY

You know what to do: Write a short poem about whatever comes to mind.

Copy the final version onto a loose piece of paper and put it in your pocket for Future You to find on another day.

SONNET

TELEPHONE DAY

To celebrate, you just have to do what you probably do every day anyway. But let's have some fun with it. Don't just use your phone—use it to make a phone call. Whoa!

Who did you talk to on the phone today? What did you talk about?

_____

_____

_____

_____

_____

_____

_____

_____

_____

GO COMMANDO DAY

Today, go commando. That means don't wear any underwear. It'll feel so breezy and freeing! Hopefully.

Write an ode to your commando experience!

HAPFY TYPØ DSY

Hey, you up?

Yah, wanna poop over?

Oops. Today is a day to celebrate typos: Sometimes embarrassing, sometimes funny, sometimes a result of not taking your boring, required typing classes seriously enough in your youth.

What are a few typos you find yourself making over and over?

_____

_____

_____

_____

_____

_____

_____

SUPERHERO DAY

Time to celebrate all the superheroes in your life—
whether they have actual superpowers or not.

Who do you consider a superhero (and what would
their superhero name be)?

_____

_____

_____

_____

_____

_____

_____

_____

DANCE DAY

Dance your butt off today, even if it's just for a few minutes before bed. Just dance.

What's your favorite dance move? Is there a specific memory you associate with dancing?

_____

_____

_____

_____

_____

HONESTY DAY

Clearly, you need to be brutally honest all day long. Just don't get *too* brutal with your honesty.

How honest are you on a regular basis? And you'd better tell the truth!

MOTHER MAY I DAY

Today, take a moment to mull this over: What's something that you're SO happy you no longer have to ask your mother (or other parental figure) for permission to do?

_____

_____

_____

_____

_____

_____

_____

_____

_____

TRUFFLE DAY

Whether we're talking truffle chocolates or mushrooms, those things are rich.

What's the best truffle or truffle-based dish you've ever eaten? Describe all the mouth feels here.

PARANORMAL DAY

Ghosts, werewolves, and poltergeists, oh my!
Indulge your belief in all things not-exactly-of-
this-earthly-plane today. Do you believe in ghosts?
Why or why not? Have you ever had a ghostly
encounter? Describe it!

_____

_____

_____

_____

_____

_____

_____

_____

_____

_____

_____

_____

OLD PASSWORDS DAY

Conventional internet wisdom states that you should change your online passwords every 90 days or so. And you shouldn't just re-use a variation on the same password, either!

To celebrate, change your current passwords, and keep a list of your old passwords here—so you remember to never re-use them.

IT'S TIME FOR CHANGE!

CARTOONIST DAY

What's your favorite cartoon or comic strip from childhood? Do a quick sketch of yourself as you'd look if YOU were starring in that strip or cartoon!

BEVERAGE DAY

All you have to do is consume a beverage today. Which you should do anyway to, you know, avoid dehydration.

What's your ALL-TIME fave beverage and why?

_____

_____

_____

_____

_____

_____

_____

TOURISM DAY

Today, act like a tourist in your own city or town. Fanny pack 100% optional!

What touristy things have you always wanted to do but haven't gotten around to?

_____

_____

_____

_____

_____

_____

_____

HOROSCOPE DAY

Got your star chart handy? Make sure you check out what's in store for your day/week/month according to the zodiac.

What lies ahead? And how much do you trust horoscopes?

_____

_____

_____

_____

_____

_____

_____

_____

_____

_____

_____

_____

LOST SOCK MEMORIAL DAY

RIP to the lost socks of the world—and there are a ton of them. To celebrate, craft an ode to all those lost socks (and pour one out for their lonely other halves).

CLEAN UP YOUR ROOM DAY

Mo-om! Do I have to?

Spend some time today tidying up your physical space and your metaphorical space, too—your mind. Take a deep breath and clear out those mental cobwebs!

Are you naturally messy or neat? And which would you rather be?

TWILIGHT ZONE DAY

Do-do-do-do-do-do-do-do...

Indulge in your most fantastical macabre
sensibilities today.

What's the spookiest, most otherworldly TV show or
movie you've ever seen? What would you do if that
plot happened IRL?

_____

_____

_____

_____

_____

_____

LIMERICK DAY

There once was a day in mid-May...

Actually, that day is today!

Write your very own limerick here, using your name in the first line (i.e. "There once was a person named ___...").

THERE WAS AN OLD MAN
OF BLACKHEATH
WHOSE HEAD WAS ADORNED
WITH A WREATH
OF LOBSTERS AND SPICE,
PICKLED ONIONS & MICE,
THAT UNCOMMON MAN
OF BLACKHEATH.

MAKE UP A WORD DAY

Splorgtastic! Make up your own word, define it, and for extra credit, submit it to an online dictionary to see if it holds up to scrutiny.

DANCE LIKE A CHICKEN DAY

Here's hoping you've got your dancing shoes on, because giving anything less than 110% is just unacceptable.

When was the last time you did The Chicken Dance?

CHOCOLATE CHIP DAY

For the love of all that's Nestlé® Toll House®, indulge your semi-sweet tooth today!

Engage in a little thought experiment: What amount of chocolate chips is the perfect amount to exist in a chocolate chip cookie?

_____

_____

_____

_____

_____

_____

BIOGRAPHERS DAY

May we all be so famous one day (hopefully not
infamous!) that we need a biographer.

How would your biography start?

_____

_____

_____

_____

_____

_____

_____

_____

_____

_____

_____

_____

PACK RAT DAY

Calling all clutterphiles! Today is for you.

What are you totally a pack rat about that you maybe shouldn't be? Do you think you'll ever get rid of those beloved objects?

_____

_____

_____

_____

_____

_____

_____

_____

_____

_____

_____

_____

_____

PLAN TO VISIT YOUR RELATIVES DAY

IT'S BEEN TOO LONG!

Prepare all your important life updates! You just *know* those family members are going to have some questions. Starting with: Why don't you visit me more?

Which relative would you most like to visit? Start planning your trip here.

_____

_____

_____

_____

_____

BiKE TO WORK DAY

I hope the weather is good, because you're biking to work! That is if you a) can ride a bike, b) own a bike, and/or c) live close enough to your work to bike there.

Describe your daily commute. Would you bike it if you could?

_____

_____

_____

_____

_____

_____

BE A MILLIONAIRE DAY

If you had a million dollars…you'd be a millionaire.

But today, celebrate by just *imagining* that you've got millions.

What would you do or buy first if you won the lottery?

_____

_____

_____

_____

_____

_____

_____

_____

_____

_____

_____

MEMO DAY

MEMO

To: You

From: Me

Re: Memo Day

To celebrate, write a memo
to your Future Self about your day.

_____

_____

_____

_____

_____

_____

_____

_____

_____

_____

_____

MUSIC APPRECIATION DAY

La-la-la-la-la...

To celebrate, make a list of your very favorite songs here (and then play them on repeat all day long).

LUCKY PENNY DAY

There's *so* much luck waiting for you out there.
Keep your eyes peeled for lucky pennies.

What kind of luck are you hoping comes your way
today?

_____

_____

_____

_____

_____

_____

_____

_____

_____

_____

SCAVENGER HUNT DAY

Make up a random list of things and do your best to hunt them down today, even if you only have time to do a quickie scavenger hunt around your bedroom. Still totally counts.

What are you on the lookout for?

_____

_____

_____

_____

_____

_____

BROWN BAG IT DAY

Your challenge is to eat a homemade lunch today. Your wallet will definitely thank you!

If you brought your lunch to work or school in a brown paper bag every day, how much money would you save?

_____

_____

_____

_____

_____

_____

_____

_____

PAPER AiRPLANE DAY

You can start today by channeling the Wright brothers.

Make a paper airplane. Decorate it. Fly it.

And tell your most interesting flying story here.

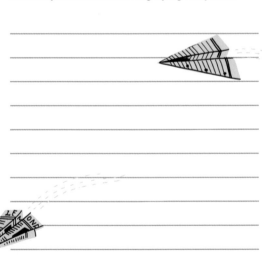

SUNSCREEN DAY

Today's an important one. Say it loud and proud:
SPF! SPF! SPF!

Recount a time when you should have worn
sunscreen here—and use it as a reminder for the
future to always slather up.

_____

_____

_____

_____

_____

_____

_____

_____

_____

HAMBURGER DAY

If you're a meat-eater, go for it today. If not, have a veggie burger!

No burger would be complete without a side. What's your favorite side dish (and why)?

_____

_____

_____

_____

_____

_____

LEARN ABOUT COMPOSTING DAY

Spend today digging in (get it?) and learning about how you can contribute to our beautiful planet.

What can you compost? What can't you? And most importantly...will you do it?

_____

_____

_____

_____

_____

WATER A FLOWER DAY

Grab your watering can and keep an eye out for thirsty flowers!

Water a flower today, literally. If you don't have access to a garden, get yourself some cut flowers. Which flower is your favorite and why?

_____

_____

_____

_____

_____

_____

SPEAK IN COMPLETE SENTENCES DAY

That made me laugh out loud!

No fragments here! Take it a step further and only express complete thoughts today—nothing half-baked allowed.

List some abbreviations that you use way too often.

_____

_____

_____

_____

_____

_____

_____

_____

FLIP A COIN DAY

Are you rooting for heads or tails?

What's the most interesting conflict you've ever resolved by flipping a coin? What conflict could you solve using this method in the near future?

LEAVE WORK EARLY DAY

Shhh, don't tell your boss. Actually, do tell your boss, because it's the best excuse ever to leave early: A totally-made-up holiday.

What would you do with all the extra time you'd gain by leaving work early?

_____

_____

_____

_____

_____

_____

_____

PEACE OUT!

REPEAT DAY

Happy Repeat Day! (Happy Repeat Day!)

That's going to get annoying. (That's going to get annoying.)

Describe one day from your past that you'd most like to repeat and why.

_____

_____

_____

_____

_____

_____

_____

_____

_____

REPEAT DAY!

CUT YOUR OWN HAIR DAY

Grab those scissors! Did you ever practice cutting hair on a doll, a pet, or yourself when you were a kid? Good! Those skills will surely be useful today.

What's the worst hairstyle you ever had? Details!

_____

_____

_____

_____

_____

_____

_____

_____

_____

_____

NO TV DAY

Television can be a great escape, but *one* day
without TV? You can definitely do it.

What did you do with all that free time? What TV
did you miss today that you'll totally have to binge
tomorrow?

_____

_____

_____

_____

_____

_____

_____

_____

_____

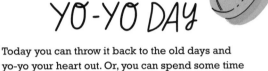

YO-YO DAY

Today you can throw it back to the old days and yo-yo your heart out. Or, you can spend some time thinking about the mental yo-yo-ing in your life...

What's something you find yourself constantly going back and forth on?

_____

_____

_____

_____

_____

_____

_____

_____

_____

_____

_____

_____

_____

TEMPORARY TATTOO DAY

Temporary tattoos are a great way to experiment with a tattoo without having to commit to one design for the rest of your life.

If you got a tattoo, what would it be and why?

BEST FRIENDS DAY

Best friends are the…well, they're the absolute best, aren't they?

Who's your BFF? Share one of your favorite bestie memories here (and then text your best friend to share the memory with them, too).

_____

_____

_____

_____

_____

_____

_____

_____

BE ST
FRIE NDS
FOR 'EVER

LiFE SOUNDTRACK DAY

Crank up the tunes! Celebrating will be a blast for all you music-lovers out there.

Craft the perfect track listing for your life here, and don't forget to include the reasoning for each song, if you're so inclined.

BALLPOINT PEN DAY

Everyone has a favorite type of pen, right?

Draw something really cute in ballpoint pen here—bonus points if you use multiple ballpoint pens in different colors!

HELP A FRIEND DAY

Get that helping hand ready. No amount of help is too small—just contribute whatever you can to a bud in need today.

Is there a specific time a friend helped you that stands out in your memory?

_____

_____

_____

_____

_____

_____

_____

_____

RED ROSE DAY

Roses are red, violets are blue…

Fill in the rest of that poem to celebrate. And if you have time, treat yourself to a beautiful red rose. Just because!

WEED YOUR GARDEN DAY

If you don't have a garden, that's okay. Just take some time today to weed your mental garden—meditate and clear out as many negative or unproductive thoughts as you can.

How do you feel after your weeding?

_____

_____

_____

_____

_____

_____

_____

_____

BODILY FUNCTION DAY

Okay, some bodily functions are…kind of gross (like burping). But they *are* necessary. #Science. So take some time today to appreciate some of your bodily functions.

Which one seems most important?

_____

_____

_____

_____

_____

_____

_____

_____

_____

BURP!

_____

_____

_____

SMILE POWER DAY

Say "cheese!" Today you get your chance to show off the power of a smile.

So smile big.

Whose smile is your favorite and why?

_____

_____

_____

_____

_____

_____

_____

HAIR DYE DAY

Have you ever dyed your hair? Have you always wanted to but you're too scared? Today's the day to try it—you can always wash it out tomorrow.

What's one way you've always dreamed of changing up your look?

_____

_____

_____

_____

_____

_____

_____

_____

_____

_____

EAT YOUR VEGETABLES DAY

Your stomach is going to be so happy today (and so are your parents!). It doesn't sound fun. But really, veggies are so good—and so good *for you*.

What's your favorite veggie dish? Describe it.

_____

_____

_____

_____

_____

SPLURGE DAY

Time to celebrate splurging, which can feel really good once in a while, whether you treat yourself to something big or something small.

What would you splurge on if you had NO spending limit?

_____

_____

_____

_____

_____

_____

KISSING DAY

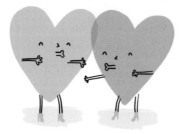

Oooooooooh! Pucker up and reminisce about your first kiss today.

Record the story here for posterity.

_____

_____

_____

_____

_____

_____

_____

_____

_____

GET OUTDOORS DAY

All you have to do to celebrate is go outside. Just once. Even for just a few minutes. You need that Vitamin D.

Are you generally an outdoor person or an indoor person? Why?

_____

_____

_____

_____

_____

_____

_____

_____

_____

_____

_____

SELFIE DAY

Hope you have a selfie stick handy (or at least a really long arm), because you've got to document the occasion. With selfies, of course!

Celebrate with some selfie love! What is your favorite thing about yourselfie?

SHELLFIE!

VOLUNTEER DAY

Today's the day to listen to that angel perched on your shoulder.

If you can't actually volunteer somewhere today, then make a resolution to volunteer in the future in whatever way you can.

What's your cause of choice?

_____

_____

_____

_____

_____

_____

VOLUNTEER

DAYDREAM DAY

Oh, what a day for a daydream…literally.

Take some time to daydream today, and recount your probably awesome daydream here.

_____

_____

_____

_____

_____

TAKE YOUR DOG TO WORK DAY

It's cool if you can't actually bring your dog to work today. Let's do a little career aptitude test to celebrate instead.

If your pet had a job, what would it be? Why? What kind of animal would be the most useful at your workplace?

STREAM OF CONCIOUSNESS DAY

To celebrate, write down all your thoughts here; don't stop to think. Just start writing and keep going until you fill up the page. Let those thoughts flow!

FORGIVENESS DAY

Today is a day to purge the grudges you usually hold all year long and think about forgiveness instead.

It's hard to forgive, but it can often help you move on.

Rather than keeping a "revenge" list, start a "forgiveness" list here.

_____

_____

_____

_____

_____

_____

SUNGLASSES DAY

All the coolest people wear their sunglasses at night. But you know what's even cooler? Wearing your sunglasses all day long, especially today!

Describe your all-time fave pair of sunglasses.

_____

_____

_____

_____

_____

_____

_____

_____

BOOK CLUB DAY

Use this day to start a book club. And while
you're at it, why not give your book club a theme?
Cookbook? Memoir? Sci-fi?

What three books have you been dying to read?
They'll be first up in your new club!

_____

_____

_____

_____

_____

_____

SECRET HANDSHAKE DAY

Secret handshakes are so cool. Make one up today, and don't forget that it's supposed to be a secret—so don't write down the moves here.

Who in your life have you shared secret handshakes with?

_____

_____

_____

_____

_____

_____

_____

_____

_____

SOCIAL MEDIA DAY

Ah, social media. We know it. It knows us. We probably love and hate it in equal measure.

What role does social media play in your life? List the pros and cons here.

CREATIVE ICE CREAM FLAVORS DAY

Ice cream is awesome and out-there flavors are even more awesome.

What's the most outlandish, creative, but also totally delicious ice cream flavor you can think of? Describe, please!

_____

_____

_____

_____

UFO DAY

Someone call the *National Inquirer*, they're probably going to want to be on high alert today.

Do you believe aliens exist? What do you think they think about humans on Earth?

_____

_____

_____

_____

_____

_____

_____

_____

_____

_____

_____

_____

_____

COMPLIMENT YOUR MIRROR DAY

Take a look in the mirror, and compliment something you see (or something you don't see, but that lies within).

Chances are you don't compliment yourself all *that* often, and hey, you need some TLC.

What's today's self-compliment?

ADVENTURE DAY

Adventure awaits around every corner.

What's the biggest adventure you've ever been on?

How can you cultivate more adventure in your everyday life?

_____

_____

_____

_____

_____

_____

_____

WORKAHOLICS DAY

Take some time today to examine your work habits.

Are you a workaholic? What are some ways you can achieve that ideal work/life balance?

NO BREAKS FOR YOU!

FRIED CHICKEN DAY

If you get a chance (and if you're not a vegetarian), grab some fried chicken today and eat up. Yum.

What other fried foods do you love? What's a fried food recipe you're *fry*ing to try?

_____

_____

_____

_____

_____

_____

_____

_____

_____

_____

_____

SUPERLATIVE DAY

Today is the day voted Most Likely to Make You Think About Yourself and Your Most Likely Tos.

To celebrate, list all of the superlatives you think you would be awarded.

_____

_____

_____

_____

_____

_____

_____

MATH 2.0 DAY

Math may not be your favorite subject or topic of conversation, but it *is* pretty important.

What are all the ways math pops up in your day-to-day life?

_____

_____

_____

_____

_____

_____

_____

_____

_____

_____

WINK DAY

Feel free to get some shut-eye today! But not that kind of shut-eye—the winking kind.

In your experience, has a wink worked to convey what you wanted it to in any particular situation?

_____

_____

_____

_____

_____

_____

_____

_____

_____

_____

BUSY DAY

Do you ever feel too busy? Like, way too busy? So busy that "busy" has become a dirty word?

Today, take a breather by treating yourself to some of your favorite indulgences, and consider how you can make your life a little less . . . you know.

_____

_____

_____

_____

_____

_____

_____

_____

_____

_____

CHEER SOMEONE UP DAY

Everyone gets bummed out sometimes, right?
Brainstorm some cheerful ideas here (and maybe
you can refer back to this list the next time you're
feeling blue).

SIMPLICITY DAY

Today, celebrating is simple.

What are some of the simple joys in your life?
And how can you bring more simplicity to your
everyday existence?

_____

_____

_____

_____

_____

_____

_____

_____

WRITE A BOOK DAY

Have you always wanted to write a book? Well, today's the day to start—or at least finally get your big idea down on paper.

What's your book idea? Outline it here.

_____

_____

_____

_____

_____

_____

_____

GLASS HOUSES DAY

Take a minute to think about hypocrisy and its role in your life. People in glass houses shouldn't throw stones and all that.

What's something that you might've been a teeny bit hypocritical about in the past?

_____

_____

_____

_____

_____

_____

_____

GIVE SOMETHING AWAY DAY

Whether it's a physical something or an intangible something (like a compliment), celebrate today by giving something away.

What'd you give away? How'd it feel?

_____

_____

_____

_____

_____

_____

_____

_____

_____

_____

FREE HUGS!

TO-DO LIST DAY

Time to get organized! What's on your to-do list for today? What about tomorrow?

Don't forget to cross tasks out as you complete them. That's half the fun!

_____

_____

_____

_____

_____

_____

_____

_____

_____

EMOJI DAY

If you were an emoji, which one would you be?
(Or would you be an emoji that doesn't even exist
yet, you unique being?)

Draw a quick sketch of yourself as an emoji here.

SOUR PUSS DAY

Celebrating grumpiness might seem weird, but you have to indulge sometimes. What makes you especially, uncharacteristically grumpy?

Can you reframe these things so they don't cause you such unhappiness?

_____

_____

_____

_____

_____

_____

_____

_____

_____

_____

_____

STICK YOUR TONGUE OUT DAY

Stick out your tongue, right here, right now. Then, take a moment to consider what in your life you'd like to metaphorically stick your tongue out at— AKA, who or what would you love to tell to buzz off?

_____

_____

_____

_____

_____

_____

_____

_____

_____

_____

MOON DAY

Celebrate the moon by giving it
a little wave when you see it tonight
—it's pretty cool, after all.

If you could leave one thing on the moon for future
moonwalkers to find, what would it be and why?

_____

_____

_____

_____

_____

_____

_____

_____

_____

_____

JUNK FOOD DAY

Junk food isn't really good for you, per se, but it sure does taste awesome. Must be all the sugar and/or grease.

What are your favorite junk foods? Rank the top ten here.

_____

_____

_____

_____

_____

_____

_____

HAMMOCK DAY

Relaxation is the name of the game today.

What would be the most relaxing way to spend your day? Describe the imagined experience (maybe just visualizing it will help you relax).

_____

_____

_____

_____

_____

_____

MOVIE QUOTE DAY

We're gonna need…a bigger piece of paper.
Failure is not an option. May the force be with you
as you celebrate today!

Rank your top three favorite movies here, and
include quotes from each.

COUSINS DAY

Today is the day to celebrate the branches of your family tree! Do you have a lot of cousins? Are you close? What's your favorite cousin-related memory?

Make sure to reach out to your cousins today, just to say hi!

_____

_____

_____

_____

_____

_____

_____

_____

THREAD THE NEEDLE DAY

Think about those moments in life that require careful balance and precision. A tricky sports maneuver? Finding a solution to a seemingly unsolvable problem? Literally threading a needle to sew?

What are some of those moments in your life, and how can you "thread the needle" in each?

_____

_____

_____

_____

_____

ALL OR NOTHING DAY

Take a moment to think about the things in life that you've been waffling on. What are they?

Today is the day to make a decision: Are you all in, or all out?

DESERTED ISLAND DAY

Today, consider the age-old question: If you were stranded on a deserted island and could only bring three items with you, what would they be and why?

_____

_____

_____

_____

_____

_____

_____

_____

_____

_____

_____

RECIPE DAY

Whether you're an ace cook or not, chances are you've followed a recipe at least once in your life.

Today, celebrate Recipe Day by copying down your favorite recipe here—to make sure you *never* lose it.

_____

_____

_____

_____

_____

_____

_____

LiPSTiCK DAY

Purse those lips, baby! One of the best parts of a lipstick is its name, so today, celebrate lipstick by making up your own super creative lipstick name.

What's the name of your new lipstick? Describe the color, too.

_____

_____

_____

_____

_____

_____

_____

_____

FRIENDSHIP DAY

As the name suggests, it's the day to celebrate friendship, which is really heartwarming.

Write a silly ode to a friend of your choice today, including at least three of your favorite things about them.

_____

_____

_____

_____

_____

_____

_____

_____

_____

_____

HARRY POTTER DAY

Whip out those magic wands! Time to celebrate all things Potter (if you've never read any Harry Potter books, today is the day to start)!

Craft your own wizarding world spell here, including an explanation of what it would do, of course.

_____

_____

_____

_____

_____

_____

OOTD DAY

Why *not* catalogue your outfits (perhaps using #OOTD), right? It'll help keep things fresh and interesting—and maybe even illuminate some outfit preferences you didn't even know you had.

What have you worn over the last week?

_____

_____

_____

_____

_____

_____

_____

_____

_____

_____

_____

Coloring BOOK DAY!

Get your colored pencils, crayons, and markers ready! The world is your blank page, and who says you have to color inside the lines?

To celebrate, color anything and everything today. Including this whole page—just go for it!

GRAB SOME NUTS DAY

Grab some cashews, almonds, peanuts, etc. (and eat them—unless you're allergic). Write a quick love poem to your favorite kind of nut, here.

_____

_____

_____

_____

_____

_____

_____

_____

_____

SKiP THE SHOWER DAY

Skipping your daily shower will save water, save
time, and you'll probably smell only a little.

What do you wish you had ten—or however long
your shower actually is—extra minutes for every
single day?

_____

_____

_____

_____

_____

_____

_____

_____

_____

UNDERWEAR DAY

Under where? Under who? Whether you love or hate wearing underwear, today's the day to spare a thought for your ol' underoos.

What's your favorite pair of underwear? Come on, everyone has one pair they can't live without.

_____

_____

_____

_____

_____

_____

FRESH BREATH DAY

Grab the floss and mouthwash because you're going to want to celebrate today by getting as minty fresh as possible.

Take this opportunity to make your next dentist appointment RIGHT NOW! And write down all the pros of keeping your mouth fresh and clean.

_____

_____

_____

_____

_____

_____

_____

_____

_____

_____

iT'S NOT ABOUT YOU DAY

You're the star of the movie known as your life, right? But even so, not *everything* is about you, and today you've got to check that ego.

What are some ways you can you remind yourself every day that it's not all about you?

CAT DAY

Me-*ow*. To celebrate today, spend some time thinking about these feline friends.

What are your favorite (or least favorite) things about cats?

_____

_____

_____

_____

_____

_____

_____

_____

_____

BOOK LOVERS' DAY

Today is for all the book lovers out there—those who just can't help themselves from buying books, reading books, even sniffing books (yup, sniffing books). Why do you love books so much?

List your top ten favorite books here.

_____

_____

_____

_____

_____

_____

_____

_____

_____

_____

LAZY DAY

Today is the day to—you guessed it! —indulge in laziness. Don't put too much pressure on yourself to be productive. Take a few moments to just relax.

Keep a list here of everything you do—or don't do—during your lazy day.

_____

_____

_____

_____

_____

_____

_____

#HASHTAG DAY

Just a few years ago, who even knew what a hashtag was? And now they're #everywhere. Celebrating today is simple: Make up a witty and pithy hashtag. Get creative!

How would you describe yourself in one #hashtag?

_____

_____

_____

_____

_____

_____

_____

_____

_____

_____

MIDDLE CHILD DAY

To all the middle children out there, today is for you. Time to soak up all the attention!

What's it like to be in your spot in the family order—be it older, younger, middle, or only child?

_____

_____

_____

_____

_____

LEFT-HANDERS DAY

If you're left-handed, today is your day—own it.

Write a diary entry about your day here…using your non-dominant hand.

PROUD LEFTIE

CLICHÉ DAY

When life hands you lemons, make lemonade.

What's one cliché you're ready to retire from the cultural lexicon? And one that you think is actually underrated and could stand to be used more?

_____

_____

_____

_____

_____

_____

_____

_____

_____

TASTE BUDS DAY

Today, pick your favorite taste sensation (salty, sour, bitter, sweet, and umami) and write a love poem to it and all the flavors it brings to mind.

_____

_____

_____

_____

_____

_____

_____

_____

TELL A JOKE DAY

Tap into your funny bone—everyone has one—and tell a joke (or two, or three!). Even better if it's one you made up.

What's your all-time favorite joke?

_____

_____

_____

_____

_____

_____

_____

_____

_____

_____

THRIFT SHOP DAY

Time to dig through some of your old junk. What are some items you've been meaning to donate or throw out? What memories do they conjure up?

_____

_____

_____

_____

_____

_____

_____

_____

_____

_____

_____

_____

BAD POETRY DAY

Today, celebrate the bad poetry, instead of just casting it aside.

Write some really bad, terrible, awful poetry today. Do your worst.

PHOTO DAY

A picture is worth a thousand words.

So to celebrate today, pick one of your favorite photos and write about it here (it's okay if you can't get to 1,000 words—that *is* a lot).

_____

_____

_____

_____

_____

_____

_____

_____

_____

_____

_____

RADIO DAY

Occasional static and commercials aside, the radio can be pretty great.

If you ran a radio station, what genre of music would it play? And what would your on-air DJ name and persona be?

SENIOR CITIZENS' DAY

Time to put yourself in a senior state of mind. Take some time today to connect with the seniors in your life, if you can.

What are *you* most looking forward to in *your* golden years?

_____

_____

_____

_____

_____

_____

_____

_____

TOOTH FAIRY DAY

Do you have all of your adult teeth? Shucks.

In lieu of giving up some baby teeth, take some time to reminisce about a losing-a-tooth memory. Details, please!

RiDE THE WIND DAY

Okay, the wind doesn't actually run, but how would you like it if you could run like the wind, metaphorically? In what life situation would that idiomatic skill most come in handy?

_____

_____

_____

_____

_____

_____

_____

_____

RIP PLUTO DAY

Remember when Pluto was a planet, then wasn't a planet, then was a planet again?

Write a letter to Pluto, letting it know how cool you think space is, to make it feel better about the back-and-forth.

KISS AND MAKE UP DAY

Take some time today to make up with someone—
isn't it time you put all the animosity behind you?

What's the best/most meaningful "kiss and make
up" moment you've ever had?

_____

_____

_____

_____

_____

_____

_____

_____

DOG DAY

Woof, woof. Celebrate by listing your favorite (or least favorite) things about dogs here.

(Bonus: Flip back to August 8th—which animal had more "favorite" traits listed—cats or dogs?)

JUST BECAUSE DAY

You don't always need a million reasons to justify your thoughts or actions. What did you do today, just because?

_____

_____

_____

_____

_____

_____

_____

BLACK TIE DAY

Have you ever gotten dressed up—like, really, really dressed up? What piece of clothing makes you feel like a million bucks? Or would you rather be in sweats?

_____

_____

_____

_____

_____

_____

_____

_____

_____

_____

CARBON FOOTPRINT DAY

Take a few moments to think about your carbon footprint—how can you reduce it?

List some planet-saving to-dos here.

_____

_____

_____

_____

_____

_____

FRANKENSTEIN DAY

Spend a few seconds today imagining yourself and those around you as Frankenstein's monster.

If you could Frankenstein any personality traits and add them to yourself, what traits would you want?

_____

_____

_____

_____

_____

_____

_____

_____

EAT OUTSIDE DAY

If the weather permits, eat outside today. But not on the ground! Picnic Day is a completely different day.

What's your favorite outdoor spot to eat? What are the best and worst parts about eating outside?

NO RHYME NO REASON DAY

Write the most nonsensical poem you can think of today—and no rhyming allowed. The less sense it makes and the less rhyming it is, the better.

_____

_____

_____

_____

_____

BLUEBERRY iCE POP DAY

Today's mission: Find a refreshing blueberry
popsicle and eat it. If not blueberry, what's your
favorite ice pop flavor?

What else cools you down on a hot day?

_____

_____

_____

_____

_____

_____

_____

_____

_____

_____

OH YES!
BLUEBERRY
GOOD-
NESS!

SKYSCRAPER DAY

What location in your town or city gives an aerial view of your surroundings? Go there today, if you can.

How can changing your physical perspective change your mental perspective?

_____

_____

_____

_____

_____

_____

_____

_____

_____

_____

_____

NEWSPAPER CARRIER DAY

Find a newspaper carrier (you might have to get up real early for that!) and thank them for the work they are doing to keep print media alive.

What's your favorite newspaper section? Write a headline for it based on how your week is going.

_____

_____

_____

_____

_____

_____

_____

_____

_____

_____

_____

CHEESE PIZZA DAY

Eat tons and tons of pizza today—so much that you might *turn into* a slice of pizza yourself.

What's your favorite pizza-related memory? Was it love at first bite?

_____

_____

_____

_____

_____

_____

_____

_____

_____

'SUP HOME SLICE!

READ A BOOK DAY

Nerds, rejoice! You should obviously celebrate by reading a book.

Copy down the first sentence you read today below.

_____

_____

_____

_____

_____

_____

_____

_____

BEER LOVER'S DAY

Try some new beers, or root beers, if you can't legally drink beer!

Write down your favorites so you remember for the next time you want a refreshing drink.

_____

_____

_____

_____

_____

_____

_____

_____

_____

_____

GRANDPARENTS' DAY

Holy senior citizens, Batman! Celebrate today by calling up a grandparent to say hi, writing a letter to a grandparent, or just reminiscing about one (or two, or three, or four) of your grandparents.

What's your favorite grandparent-related memory?

_____

_____

_____

_____

_____

_____

_____

_____

_____

_____

_____

_____

TEDDY BEAR DAY

Channel your inner stuffed animal lover and indulge in some of your childhood memories today.

Draw a picture of your favorite teddy bear here.

SWAP IDEAS DAY

Whether it's during a meeting, a casual conversation, or a chat with a friend, don't be shy today—give away some ideas! And collect some, too!

What's useful about exchanging ideas? Were you inspired today?

_____

_____

_____

_____

_____

_____

MAKE YOUR BED DAY

Today, do like you were always told as a kid, and make your bed. It may not be fun, but it just *looks* so good.

What's the best thing about getting into a pristinely made bed at the end of the day?

_____

_____

_____

_____

_____

_____

_____

_____

_____

_____

_____

MiNDFULNESS DAY

Today, be extra mindful of yourself, your actions, your surroundings, and others.

Spend a few moments reflecting on how to be more mindful day-to-day, and write down a few mindfulness resolutions here.

_____

_____

_____

_____

_____

_____

_____

_____

POSITIVE THINKING DAY

Keep that brain turned on and whirring, because you're going to need some brain power to celebrate today right. Think positive—even when things go wrong.

What are some of the silver linings you sought out—and found—today?

GO STREAKING DAY

Streak if you can today! Even if it's just a quick lap around your home—still counts.

What the best thing about wearing *only* your birthday suit? How does it make you feel?

_____

_____

_____

_____

_____

_____

_____

_____

_____

_____

ONLiNE LEARNiNG DAY

Power up that internet connection (LOL, remember dial-up?). You've got some fact-finding to do.

What did you learn online today? Transcribe it here so you never un-learn it.

PLAY-DOH DAY

Throwback alert! You probably haven't played with Play-Doh all that recently, but get into the spirit of today by reaching back in your memory…

What's the best thing about Play-Doh? The feel? The smell?

_____

_____

_____

_____

_____

_____

_____

GiRLFRIENDS DAY

Today, celebrate the best girlfriends in your life.

What would you do on a girlfriends-only weekend?
Brainstorm an itinerary here (and then make it
happen!).

REGRET DAY

Normally, it's better to leave regrets where they belong—in the past—but today, indulge in some reflection (and *then* toss those regrets behind you).

What's your biggest regret in life (and how will you move on, starting today)?

_____

_____

_____

_____

_____

_____

_____

_____

_____

_____

TALK LiKE A PiRATE DAY

Arrrr, you know what to do, matey.

Write a diary entry about your day—but in pirate-speak, exclusively.

_____

_____

_____

_____

_____

_____

_____

_____

_____

_____

PUNCH DAY

Gloves? Check. Punching bag? Check.

Instead of going around punching everyone and everything, spend a minute working out your anger on the page. What in your life makes you feel like throwing a wild punch? And is there another way you could resolve that feeling?

MiNiATURE GOLF DAY

To celebrate today, all you have to do is head outside and play some mini-golf.

If you can't, make up a creative mini-golf hole obstacle here (remember that a windmill always makes things harder!).

DEAR DIARY DAY

Dear Diary,

The best way to celebrate today is to write a diary entry about your day, of course. But also, take a walk down memory lane and read an old diary, if you have one available.

Xoxo

CHANGE YOUR MIND DAY

Sometimes things are going to hold true for you. Other times, you're going to change your mind. One day, your favorite food is pizza; the next, it's sushi!

What's something you've changed your mind about recently?

_____

_____

_____

_____

_____

_____

PUNCTUATION DAY

Calling all exclamation points and ellipses!

What's your favorite punctuation and why? List all the awesome ways you use it in your everyday life.

_____

_____

_____

_____

_____

_____

_____

_____

_____

_____

_____

COMIC BOOK DAY

Whether or not you've ever read a comic book before now, you can participate in celebrating today.

If you could be the star of a comic book, what would your character be like? What would your comic book be called?

_____

_____

_____

_____

_____

LOVE NOTE DAY

Get all your schmoopy, mushy, gushy feelings to the surface. To celebrate today, write a love note—to anyone or anything—here, even if you never plan to deliver it to the object of your affection.

_____

_____

_____

_____

_____

_____

_____

_____

MEDITATE DAY

Ommmm...

If you're new to the practice of meditation, just try it out, even for a few minutes. All you need is a little peace and quiet.

How do you feel after dabbling in meditation?

_____

_____

_____

_____

_____

STUPID QUESTION DAY

You know what they say: There are no stupid questions. But what's one stupid question you've always wanted to ask? Write it down here. Feel free to look up the answer and record that here, too. Now you never have to wonder again!

_____

_____

_____

_____

_____

_____

_____

_____

COFFEE DAY

Drink coffee. Lots of it. If you've never had coffee before, today's the day to try it. And decaf is allowed!

What role does coffee play in your life, and what are all the things you love or hate about it?

_____

_____

_____

_____

_____

_____

_____

CHEWING GUM DAY

Chomp, chomp! Aside from celebrating by chewing, chewing, chewing today, invent the wildest gum flavor you can imagine, and describe it here (bonus points if you design a funky label, too!).

HOMEMADE COOKIE DAY

Calling all cookie monsters…you do *not* want to miss out on all this deliciousness. To celebrate, make some cookies, eat them, rinse, and repeat.

Are you all about homemade or store bought? Why?

_____

_____

_____

_____

_____

_____

NAME YOUR CAR DAY

If you name your pet and your toys…why not name your car?

If you have a car, what's its name? And if you don't… well, what would you name your car if you *did* have one?

_____

_____

_____

_____

_____

_____

PEP TALK DAY

Everyone needs a good, ol' fashioned pep talk now and then. Why wait around for someone else to do the pepping?

Give yourself a pep talk, right here, right now.

_____

_____

_____

_____

_____

_____

TACO DAY

Today is the day to celebrate everyone's favorite tortilla-wrapped food: Tacos! Celebrating is easy—gorge yourself on tacos until you can taco no more. Don't forget the salsa!

How do you love tacos? Count the ways.

_____

_____

_____

_____

_____

_____

DO SOMETHING NICE DAY

Today is the day to show your nice side. To celebrate, do something nice for someone— whether it's a big something or a small something. It all counts!

How did doing good deeds make you feel?

_____

_____

_____

_____

_____

_____

_____

_____

_____

MAD HATTER DAY

A very merry Mad Hatter Day to you! And you, and you, and you!

Channel your very best Mad Hatter today and celebrate something totally random and out there (an un-birthday, perhaps?).

What are some made-up traditions in your life?

CARD-MAKING DAY

To celebrate today, make any kind of card—greeting card, postcard, business card…they're all fair game. Just make one and then give it away or keep it to yourself for decoration.

What's your favorite type of card to receive?

_____

_____

_____

_____

_____

_____

_____

SELF-IMPROVEMENT DAY

If you can't be honest with yourself, who *can* you be honest with? Take some time today to look inside and see where there's room for improvement.

Make some self-improvement goals—and try to stick to 'em.

_____

_____

_____

_____

_____

_____

_____

SPELLING BEE DAY

Get that brain ready and transport yourself back to third grade. S-p-e-l-l-i-n-g is the name of the game.

To celebrate, think about the handful of words you can never seem to spell correctly. Pick three and write them down here, over and over, to practice spelling them right. Fill the page—voilà! You'll almost certainly have them committed to memory.

_____

_____

_____

_____

_____

_____

_____

CAKE DECORATING DAY

To celebrate today, you should decorate a cake—but in case you don't have the time or ingredients, indulge in a little imaginary baking time.

If you *were* to decorate a cake today, what would it look like?

IT'S MY PARTY DAY

Take some time today to plan a party for any reason at all. A recent accomplishment? Your half-birthday? Perhaps you just want to celebrate the small things you do every day—like brushing your teeth or remembering to lock your front door behind you.

All of these are valid reasons to throw a party! Jot down some ideas for celebrating yourself here.

_____

_____

_____

_____

FRUSTRATION DAY

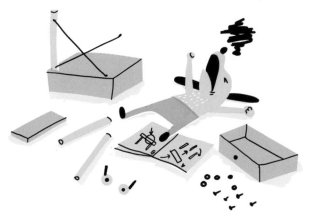

Use this space to describe something that's frustrated you recently (maybe writing about it will help you find a solution or put it behind you).

_____

_____

_____

_____

_____

_____

NO BRA DAY

To celebrate today, go commando on top—ditch the brassiere. (If you don't normally wear a bra, then just keep doin' what you're doin'.)

What are the pros and cons of going braless? Are you done with bras for good?

_____

_____

_____

_____

_____

_____

_____

HOME MOVIE DAY

Spend a few moments today making your own home movie (any recording device will do). What did you record?

Describe it here—and include the date and time, for posterity!

_____

_____

_____

_____

_____

_____

_____

_____

_____

GROUCH DAY

You have permission to indulge your grouchiness all day long. Wake up on the wrong side of the bed. Hate on everything.

Now get any grouch out of your system and onto paper so you can start fresh tomorrow!

I HATE EVERYONE!

DICTIONARY DAY

Flip through a dictionary (or browse one online) and find a word you've never heard before. Commit the word and its definition to memory, and try to use it in a sentence tomorrow. Look how much you're learning!

What's the word, hummingbird? And the definition?

_____

_____

_____

_____

_____

_____

_____

AM·PHIS·BAE·NA
/amfəs'bēnə
noun
A LEGENDARY SERPENT
WITH A HEAD ON
EACH END.

WEAR SOMETHING GAUDY DAY

It's time to dig out your tackiest, loudest, busiest
clothing from the depths of your closet. You know
what to do.

Describe—or sketch, if you feel so inclined—your
gaudy outfit of the day here.

UNICORN DAY

Today is the day to celebrate what makes you
the unique unicorn you are. So what is it—big or
small—that makes you, you? Go into detail here.

_____

_____

_____

_____

_____

_____

_____

_____

_____

_____

_____

_____

_____

EVALUATE YOUR LiFE DAY

Okay, evaluating your life is kind of a huge task to accomplish in a day. To get started, think about what your goals were five years ago. Are you living that life? Do you still want that life? What do you want for the *next* five years?

NAVEL

SLOTH DAY

Act super sloth-y today—meaning, take your time.
Move slowly. Think of today as a forced reminder
not to rush through life.

What are the benefits of slowing down?

_____

_____

_____

_____

_____

_____

_____

_____

_____

COUNT YOUR BUTTONS DAY

There are two ways to celebrate today.

1: Literally: How many buttons are on your person right now?

2: Figuratively: What are the buttons (aka pet peeves) you have that people just seem to push again and again?

_____

_____

_____

_____

_____

CAPS LOCK DAY

CAPS LOCK IS BASICALLY THE TYOPGRAPHIC EQUIVALENT OF SHOUTING. EASY ON THE EYES, RIGHT?

TO CELEBRATE, WRITE A DIARY ENTRY ABOUT YOUR DAY HERE—IN ALL CAPS, OF COURSE.

TV TALK SHOW HOST DAY

Pretend you're a TV talk show host today. If you could interview any person, living or dead, who would it be and what's the one question you're dying to ask them?

_____

_____

_____

_____

_____

_____

_____

_____

ESP DAY

Have you ever wondered if you might be just a little bit psychic? Today is the day to lean into that.

If you *were* in possession of extrasensory perception, what would you do with that newfound power?

_____

_____

_____

_____

_____

_____

_____

_____

PUNK FOR A DAY DAY

Time to get punky! Listen to punk music, dress in punk style, just get really punk and anti-establishment today.

What's the most punk thing about you?

_____

_____

_____

_____

_____

_____

_____

_____

_____

_____

_____

PUMPKIN DAY

Pumpkin pie, pumpkin soup, pumpkin spice lattes...today is the day to celebrate all that, and more. Have your fill of pumpkin today, and then expand the fall-themed celebrations here.

What are your favorite fall activities?

FACE YOUR FEAR DAY

Today is the day. You can do it. You know you can.

Whatever your fear is (Flying? Spiders? The undead?), it's time to face it and maybe even conquer it once and for all.

What's got you so scared? And how will you get over it?

_____

_____

_____

_____

_____

_____

_____

_____

PUN DAY

Get those pun guns ready! Your celebration instructions: Craft the cheesiest pun you can think of—one that's really goud-a—here. The punnier, the better!

_____

_____

_____

_____

_____

_____

_____

_____

SAY HELLO DAY

Oh, hello! To celebrate today just…say hello. To anyone and everyone. Why not make the world a friendlier place for at least one day? You might like it.

What was the last conversation you had with a complete stranger?

_____

_____

_____

_____

_____

_____

_____

DOUBLE-CHECK DAY

Spend some time with your Type-A side today and make sure you double-check all your work today—how else will you avoid mistakes?

Keep the list of things to double-check here—so you don't miss anything!

KNOCK-KNOCK JOKES DAY

Knock-knock!
Who's there?
Knock-knock.
Knock-knock…who?
Knock-Knock Jokes Day!

Celebrate the knock-knock joke all day today. Tell 'em, answer 'em, and best of all—write your own.

_____

_____

_____

_____

_____

SELF-PORTRAIT DAY

To celebrate today, think outside the box a bit—
instead of drawing a self-portrait, create one using
words. Meaning, pick the most accurate adjectives
to describe YOU and list them.

SUPER-
CALIFRAG-
ILISTIC-
EXPIAL-
IDOCIOUS!

NON-FICTION DAY

Check your wild imagination at the door and take a look at the real world around you. Read some non-fiction today! Or at least come up with a non-fiction reading list, curated around the topic that interests you most. Why this topic?

_____

_____

_____

_____

_____

_____

_____

_____

ALL ABOUT AH-NOLD

WEIGHTLIFTING + YOU

THE HISTORY OF BODY BUILDING

THINK **BIG** BODY-BUILDING BASICS

SANDWICH DAY

Which 'wich will you choose to celebrate today?
Why not celebrate them all?

Create your ideal sandwich and list the ingredients
here. Yum!

_____

_____

_____

_____

_____

STRESS AWARENESS DAY

Life is full of stress. Take a few minutes today to
zero in on all the things—big and small—that stress
you out.

What are these stressors and how can you cope?
Brainstorm some tactics here.

DONUT DAY

Oh, those round, frosted, airy treats! Make sure you eat at least one donut today.

And write an ode to your favorite doughy treat here.

_____

_____

_____

_____

_____

_____

_____

_____

BOSS DAY

To celebrate today, take a few moments to think about one aspect of your life that you want to become the boss of. What is it? And how will you achieve total bossdom?

THE BUCK STOPS HERE

PATTERNS DAY

Today's mission: Turn your keen eye on the world around you. Patterns are everywhere! Taking the time to notice them can make your day a little brighter and a little more inspirational.

Where did you see or notice patterns today? Describe them here.

_____

_____

_____

_____

_____

TONGUE TWISTER DAY

Has *anyone* ever been able to answer: "How much would a woodchuck chuck if a woodchuck could chuck wood?"

To celebrate today, come up with an elaborate tongue twister about yourself.

_____

_____

_____

_____

_____

_____

_____

_____

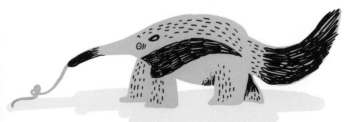

CHAOS NEVER DIES DAY

A little bit of chaotic unrest can be good for the soul
(and helps make sure you don't get bored).

How are you an agent of chaos in your everyday
life?

FORGET-ME-NOT DAY

Forget *me* not? Forget YOU not! What's the one thing that you want people to remember about you forever?

Write a note to the world that reveals your legacy.

_____

_____

_____

_____

_____

_____

FORGET
ME NOT!

NEWSLETTER DAY

Do you send out a periodic newsletter to all your friends and family to keep them up-to-date on your life? Why not start now? Everyone is probably wondering...

If you were to send out a Life Newsletter today, what would it say?

_____

_____

_____

_____

_____

_____

_____

_____

_____

_____

_____

HAPPY HOUR DAY

If you're of age, celebrate with a few adult beverages. If not, pick any hour of the day and use that time to focus on what makes you happy.

Keep a running list of all those happy-making things here. (And maybe make this "happy hour" thing a daily tradition, hmm?)

SADIE HAWKINS DAY

Ah, Sadie Hawkins—a badass lady who wasn't afraid to go for what she wanted. She was so inspiring that she got a whole high school dance tradition named after her. #Goals

To celebrate, unabashedly go after what you want, and keep a list of those wants here.

_____

_____

_____

_____

_____

_____

PICKLE DAY

Celebrating today is simple: Eat a pickle and then get to work brainstorming ways to get out of a pickle you're in right now.

_____

_____

_____

_____

_____

_____

_____

_____

PICKLE
IN A PICKLE!

_____

_____

_____

CLEAN OUT YOUR REFRIGERATOR DAY

OMG, it's everyone's favorite day of the year! Get out the rubber gloves and the baking soda: It's cleaning time.

What's the grossest thing you've ever found in the fridge? Details!

FAST FOOD DAY

We all have a guilty pleasure fast food love.
What's yours?

Rank your top five favorite fast foods here.

_____

_____

_____

_____

_____

_____

_____

_____

_____

TAKE A HiKE DAY

Take a hike today and breathe in that fresh air. Or, if hiking isn't your style, treat today as an opportunity tell someone or something to take a hike and get outta your life. Sometimes that's necessary.

Who or what doesn't belong in your life right now?

_____

_____

_____

_____

_____

_____

_____

_____

OCCULT DAY

Take a few minutes to ponder the seemingly unexplainable, the occult. If you could put a spell on anyone, what spell would it be and WHO would you cast it on?

_____

_____

_____

_____

_____

_____

_____

_____

_____

_____

_____

_____

BAD DAY DAY

Sometimes you just have a bad day. And that's okay—not every day has to be sunshine and sparkles. Even if today ends up being a great day, recall your most recent bad day below.

_____

_____

_____

_____

_____

_____

_____

_____

_____

_____

_____

ABSURDITY DAY

Take some time to notice all the absurd stuff around you: The unreasonable, the ridiculous, the illogical! Absurdity: It's everywhere!

Below, relay the details of the most absurd situation you've ever been in.

_____

_____

_____

_____

_____

_____

ENTREPRENEURS' DAY

Entrepreneurs get to see their ideas realized, to be in charge, and to risk it all in the hope of a big reward down the line. Celebrate entrepreneurs today by preparing to be one!

What's an invention or business idea you've been dreaming about?

_____

_____

_____

_____

_____

_____

GO FOR A RIDE DAY

Horseback? Magic carpet? Old timey train? Go for any kind of ride you can today.

What's your favorite thing about traveling?

BiNGE WATCH DAY

Today is the perfect day to cozy up and press "play." Text your friends for their streaming passwords and then: Watch. Watch. Watch!

What do you rewatch over and over and what's on your to-binge list?

_____

_____

_____

_____

_____

CELEBRATE YOUR UNIQUE TALENT DAY

What makes you special? Well, probably a lot of things, but today is all about that unique thing *you* can do that others can't.

What is your special talent? Describe!

_____

_____

_____

_____

_____

_____

SHOPPING REMINDER DAY

Let today serve as your reminder to shop for the things you need, big and small: A holiday present for your grandma. A new tube of toothpaste. Socks!

Keep track of your shopping list here (so you have no excuse!).

PHILOSOPHIZE DAY

Whether you consider yourself the next Socrates or not, you've probably thought about the nature of existence at *least* once in your life.

What's your philosophy? What's the meaning of life (easy question)?

_____

_____

_____

_____

_____

_____

_____

_____

_____

_____

SURPRISE DAY

To celebrate today, do something to surprise yourself—eat something new; change up your stagnant bedtime routine; or call someone you thought you'd written out of your life for good.

What steps can you take to keep mixing things up more often?

_____

_____

_____

_____

_____

_____

_____

_____

_____

_____

SHUT UP DAY

Shut *up*. Shut up! SHUT UP—even if just for a few minutes. Revel in your own silence.

What crosses your mind when you aren't thinking about what you'll say next?

_____

_____

_____

_____

_____

_____

_____

_____

_____

_____

FAN FICTION DAY

Today, celebrate being a fan by writing some unique fan fiction—that means taking something you're a fan of (book, movie, what have you) and running with it in a new direction. *Pride and Prejudice* meets *Moby Dick*? *Little Women* if Beth lived? It's all up to you!

_____

_____

_____

_____

_____

_____

_____

_____

_____

_____

_____

_____

STAY HOME BECAUSE YOU'RE WELL DAY

Sick day, shmick day. Everyone deserves to stay home when they aren't hacking up gallons of phlegm once in a while.

What will you do with this gift of a day? Plan your carefree itinerary here.

_____

_____

_____

POWER SUIT!

_____

_____

_____

_____

_____

_____

NOSTALGIA DAY

The first day of the last month of the year is the perfect time to take a look back at your year—flip through this journal if it helps.

What are you feeling most nostalgic about?

_____

_____

_____

_____

_____

_____

_____

_____

MiNiMALiST DAY

In keeping with the minimalist theme of today, describe your day—what you want from it or what happened during it—in as few words as possible.

MAKE A GIFT DAY

Instead of buying your gifts all the time, why not DIY? What gift—be it for the December holidays, your BFF's birthday, or your anniversary—could you make yourself? Brainstorm here, and then…get to work!

_____

_____

_____

_____

_____

BREATHE IN, BREATHE OUT DAY

All you need to do today is breathe in and breathe out, and repeat. It's particularly helpful if you do it during a moment of stress or anxiety.

What are other situations in which you could employ this technique?

SCENTED CANDLE DAY

Love them or hate them, there's no denying—
scented candles can be, um, overpowering.

What's one scent you'd love to infuse in a candle to
fill a room?

_____

_____

_____

_____

_____

_____

_____

_____

_____

ETIQUETTE DAY

Emily Post would say to always be as polite as possible and observe the correct etiquette in every situation you're in.

But, not all of the traditional etiquette rules apply to modern life. What etiquette customs would you erase from current society?

_____

_____

_____

_____

_____

_____

LETTER WRITING DAY

Stretch those fingers because today you're writing a letter by hand. No keyboards allowed.

Write any kind of letter you want here, and no pressure to send it if you're not ready to share all those #feelings.

_____

_____

_____

_____

_____

_____

_____

_____

_____

I'M COMING OUT,
I WANT THE WORLD TO KNOW...

TiME TRAVELER DAY

"BRB, just gotta jet off to the 1920s real quick!" This is what you'll tell your boss when they ask why you're running out of work dressed as a flapper.

Or you can use this space to describe which time period you'd most want to travel to and why.

_____

_____

_____

_____

_____

_____

_____

_____

_____

_____

_____

SiNG EVERYTHING DAY

La-la-la-la-la…sing it loud, sing it proud! Literally.
Sing it. Everything. All of it.

What's your favorite thing about singing out loud
when you're all by yourself? And what's your go-to
tune to sing along to?

_____

_____

_____

_____

_____

_____

_____

_____

_____

_____

DEWEY DECIMAL DAY

Today is the day to celebrate that infamous library shelving system you know and love!

How organized are you? Do you like sorting and compartmentalizing, or do you prefer to function under what others (like Melvil Dewey) might perceive as chaos?

_____

_____

_____

_____

_____

_____

914.8
K14R

MOYLE, PETER
Fish, an Enthusiast's Guide
University of California Press
1993 284 pages

1. FISH   2. ICTHYOLOGY   3. BIOLOGY

Copyright 1995 $14.25

SOLITUDE DAY

All you need to do to celebrate today is find a place where you can be by yourself.

Just relax and enjoy the solitude. What are some ways you can find moments of solitude in your everyday, hectic, über-connected life?

_____

_____

_____

_____

_____

_____

_____

_____

SMELL DAY

Today you'll need your nose in tip-top condition.

To properly celebrate, take a big whiff of everything around you, and record all the smells you smell here. Pick one of the scents and go into descriptive detail—what's so nice (or terrible) about it?

COCOA DAY

Even if it's not cold where you are, you can still participate—all you have to do (aside from drinking a giant mug of hot cocoa) is record your absolute favorite cocoa recipe here.

_____

_____

_____

_____

_____

_____

_____

_____

_____

_____

SARCASM DAY

To celebrate today, let your sarcastic side shine—
you know you want to—even if you're not typically a
sarcastic person.

What are the pros and cons of being sarcastic?

_____

_____

_____

_____

_____

_____

_____

NICE SWEATER.

UNDERDOG DAY

Today's the day to celebrate anyone who has ever had the odds stacked against them in any way.

Celebrate underdogs everywhere by recounting a time when you were the underdog but persevered and triumphed.

_____

_____

_____

_____

_____

_____

_____

_____

_____

_____

_____

GO FOR IT DAY

Think about something you've been wanting to do all year long—and go for it. Seriously, just go for it. What have you got to lose?

What are you going for and how will you do it?

GLITTER DAY

To celebrate today, throw glitter on anything and everything. And if you don't want to glitter-bomb your whole life, engage in a little lighthearted revenge plotting here: whose life *would* you like to cover in glitter?

_____

_____

_____

_____

_____

_____

INVENT A DRINK DAY

All drinks were invented by someone—and today's your chance to invent your very own, alcoholic or non-alcoholic. Invent a drink (and you should probably taste test it)! Don't forget to give it a fun name. Bonus points for puns.

UGLY SWEATER DAY

Today's the one day a year you can bust out your ugliest sweater and rock it with abandon. So wear the ugliest sweater you can find and then sketch a picture of it in all its ugly glory.

SECRET DAY

Whether or not you're good at keeping them, today is the day to celebrate secrets. Exciting secrets, devious secrets, this-secret-will-totally-change-your-life secrets—they're all fair game.

Write down a secret you're currently keeping here.

_____

_____

_____

_____

_____

_____

_____

_____

_____

BAD MOOD DAY

Today, let whatever's causing your holiday season crankiness to flow freely. Annoying songs? No party plans? Too many party plans? Get all your holiday-related unhappiness out on the page here. Free-write your humbugness (maybe it'll make you feel better)!

PREDICT THE FUTURE DAY

Okay, no one can *really* predict the future, but it's
fun to give it some thought. To celebrate today, give
it your best shot: What does the future hold?

LiMBO DAY

There are two ways to celebrate today. One, do the limbo! Two, think about what it means to be in limbo.

How are you in limbo in some aspect of your life right now and how can you change that?

_____

_____

_____

_____

_____

_____

ALL-NiGHTER DAY

To celebrate today, pull an all-nighter, of course.
Seriously, no sleep allowed.

But also, write down all the things that keep you up
at night, and also your tried-and-true remedies for
falling asleep.

FANTASY DAY

Today, take some time to indulge in a fantasy, even if you can't fully realize it right now.

What's your fantasy of choice?

_____

_____

_____

_____

_____

_____

HEADLINE DAY

It's time to think about the year, the month, the day you've just had—and come up with a creative line than encompasses your experience.

What's the headline that best sums up your life right now?

_____

_____

_____

_____

NO INTERRUPTIONS DAY

To celebrate today, block out a chunk of time, even a few minutes, where you'll be able to free write here without any interruptions. None!

Are you an interruptor, or more of a thoughtful observer?

CARD PLAYING DAY

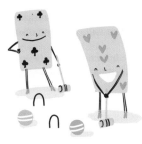

Solitaire, Poker, Gin Rummy, Go Fish—been there, done that. Celebrating today by playing one of those old games is easy and fun, but you can also celebrate by reminiscing about your favorite childhood card games here.

_____

_____

_____

_____

_____

_____

_____

TiCK-TOCK DAY

The month is almost over and the year is nearly finished. Let the final countdown begin!

To celebrate today, make a list year of all the things you want to accomplish in the last few days of the year.

_____

_____

_____

_____

_____

_____

_____

_____

_____

_____

_____

PROCRASTINATION DAY

Normally, procrastinating wouldn't be something you want to celebrate, but today—the penultimate day of the year—make a list of all the things you procrastinated on this year.

How can you do better and avoid procrastinating next year?

_____

_____

_____

_____

_____

_____

_____

_____

_____

_____

TK152 OVERCOMING
M13 PROCRASTINATION
AUTHOR BEBE BANKS
DATE ISSUED TO RET.
9/1   5/1
OVERDUE

MAKE UP YOUR MIND DAY

To celebrate the last day of the year, make up your mind about something you want to work on or learn or do next year. Just one thing. And write it down here so you can start next year on a definitive note.

_____

_____

_____

_____

_____

_____

_____

_____

_____

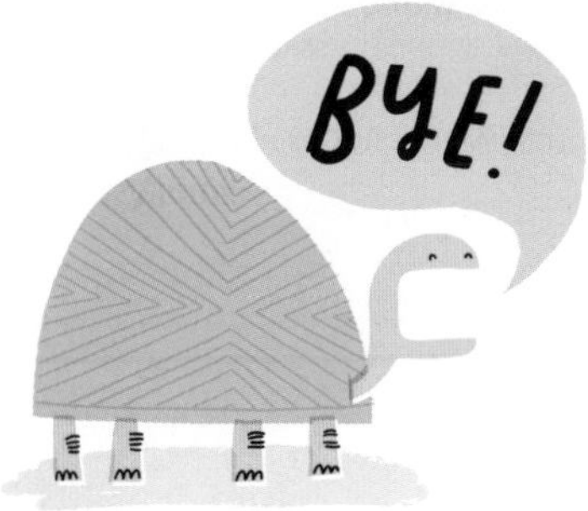
BYE!

Designer: Hana Anouk Nakamura

ISBN: 978-1-4197-3227-0

Printed and bound in China

10 9 8 7 6 5 4 3 2

Abrams Noterie products are available at special discounts
when purchased in quantity for premiums and promotions
as well as fundraising or educational use. Special editions
can also be created to specification. For details, contact
specialsales@abramsbooks.com or the address below.

ABRAMS The Art of Books
195 Broadway, New York, NY 10007
abramsbooks.com